Start a Career in
(Lazy Design
by
Brent Knowles

\#
PUBLISHED BY:
YourOtherMind Media

Learn more about the Lazy Designer series, including news on upcoming books at lazydesigner.brentknowles.com
Discover other titles by **Brent Knowles** at http://www.amazon.com/Brent-Knowles/e/B0035WW7OW

Preface

Introduction

If you love building videogames and aspire towards a career in videogame development I can relate. I spent my childhood writing stories, creating imaginary worlds and building games but never thought a career in the industry would be possible. It just seemed too *impossible.*

I was wrong.

What to Expect

I had the pleasure of spending a decade working on top rated role-playing games with the games developer BioWare. I would like to share that experience with you.

Who is this book for?

This book is geared primarily towards those looking to start a career in the games industry. Specifically the book is about obtaining a design position (writer, level designer, game system designer) but the text should be of use to anyone entering the industry.

Practical advice on how to enter the industry leads into an exploration of what a bright and shiny new employee might expect in their early years in the games industry.

> *Later books will focus on design specializations, improving quality assurance, becoming a manager and other facets that I believe will be of more value to industry veterans.*

This is not a book with any tricks or magical techniques that will make you a better videogame developer. I am a practical designer and in my time with BioWare I built high quality video games in reasonable time frames and with reasonable resources. This is not a design book. It is a book about becoming a capable designer and an asset to your team and to the company.

I will not go into great detail on how to design a game, the components used to build games, how game engines work, or even how to develop an emotionally engaging storyline from start to finish.

To be blunt I learned all those skills after I already had started employment with BioWare. Certainly my fiction writing and gaming experiences had prepared me with the basic skills I needed but I was a raw recruit.

I have since attended lectures and read several manuals on various design philosophies (some of which are referenced at the end of this book) and expanded my skills. But my practical work methodology and never-ending eagerness to learn is why I was constantly given new responsibilities early in my career and why I became a lead designer not long after starting work with BioWare.

There are no shortcuts when creating great games but you can improve your own skills by understanding how others, like myself, solved common problems in game development.

This book begins with a chapter on to how best prepare yourself for a videogame development career and how to find that first job. The next two chapters explore improving your skills and tackling the roadblocks you will encounter. After a discussion on how to design *fun frustrations* for players I end with a list of links to online references I have found useful in my own career.After reading this book you will know how to increase your chances of getting an interview, obtaining the job you want and excelling at the tasks given you.

I encourage you to read other design books, to master the nuts and bolts of gameplay and story and world-building. Those are important. But without a strong work ethic and the desire and ability to *improve* yourself and your project, you will not have the opportunity to put those other skills to the test.

What is a Game

At this point in most books of this nature the author usually writes a lengthly discussion of what a game is and offers some descriptions. Because there are many great books already covering that topic, I will not do so in any great detail.

Personally I think a videogame should have choices --interesting and entertaining choices and consequences for those choices. Most choices should influence the game's narrative. But not all. Some choices should simply be amusing or should help the player gain ownership of the game world they are experiencing.

About the Lazy Designer series

Throughout this work I'll make reference to other books in the *Lazy Designer series*. This is only the first book of what will eventually be five titles, each exploring a subset of the game development experience, mirroring my own career from new employee to specialist to manager. Later books will give advice on how to improve design skills, improve communication and balance work in life... all things I had to do as I moved onto my second project, the Neverwinter Nights franchise. Eventually, the final books will delve into my experiences as a design manager -- my successes and my mistakes.Before we start delving into content I would like to make a couple points clear.

- **Feedback**. I thrive on feedback. Please let me know when you find mistakes. My **Contact Page** (http://blog.brentknowles.com/contactnewsletter/) has a variety of methods to reach me. I'm eager to know if there are topics you would like to see covered in later books, discussed on my blog, or even added to a later edition of this book. I want this to be a cooperative process where I'm learning as much as you.

- **You, the Reader**. I will often delve into topics of a higher level than a new employee needs to know. I do this because this is what I am familiar with. For most of my career I was a manager. I also do it because I think it helps prepare you for when you yourself might be leading teams. Even if that is not something you aspire towards it might help you understand the influence behind the decisions that your manager makes.

- **Buyer Beware**. Most of the content in this book is available free at my website www.brentknowles.com, in the form of blog posts I made over the past few years though it has been rewritten and reorganized here.

Additionally, as mentioned previously, this is the first of a series of books. When later books are released this book's price will be reduced and perhaps eventually be set to free.I'm telling this to you now to avoid later disappointments. If you would rather not pay anything for this book its price will probably be reduced in the future. That said, I earn my living from freelance writing and if I do not have enough sales to justify distributing the later sections I will focus my attention on writing fiction instead. (If you are so inclined I have several short stories, including a Writers of the Future winning story, available online... check http://blog.brentknowles.com/bibliography/ for details.)

Why Lazy?

I believe in enhancing the work experience, no matter the task I am engaged in.

There is a time for designers to roll up their sleeves and just get the work done but when possible I think it is important that designers understand how valuable their time is. Should you waste days doing a task that could be automated and completed in a couple minutes? Doesn't it make more sense to devote your time to more creative tasks?

I believe in getting tools and procedures in place so that design effort is spent in the right way -- making the game entertaining. In that regard I am lazy. I don't want to do the hard, boring work. I want to work hard at the fun stuff.

Conventions Used in this Book

Anecdotes

Occasional anecdotes, generally from my time at BioWare, will appear formatted like this.

Notes

Important points clarifying the preceding text will be shown like this.

Reference

References to other chapters will be capitalized. For example, if you would like to read more about designing cyborg assistants, please consult CHAPTER 92.

CHAPTER 1 - Starting Your Career

A career in game development is an appealing prospect to anybody who grew up playing videogames. What else could be more satisfying? I still fondly remember my youth and staying up late playing games with friends -- discovering new worlds and characters and being astonished as the technology improved and the game experience with it. I wanted to be part of that.

In this chapter I will explore how you can prepare yourself for such a career and then discuss what you should consider as you start applying for work in the videogames industry.

How to Prepare for a Career in the Games Industry

Caution! Danger Ahead!

Before proceeding you need to decide if game development is the right choice for you. Games are fun to play but challenging and demanding to build. Sixty hour work weeks are not uncommon; some studios ask for much more than this. Many studios pay well but are located in cities that are very expensive to live in.

Do your homework on companies you think you would like to work for, especially if you have a family and/or will have to relocate. Some companies have online groups where past employees tend to congregate, you might want to check those out and ask questions.

> *Watch out for bitter apples... after leaving a company former employees can tend to focus on the unpleasant experiences. They still may have valuable advice to offer you but may package it in negativity.*

Additionally even at the best studios all designers need to be prepared to see their hard work cut. Repeatedly. Changing technology and publisher demands combined with inexperienced managers makes project management more of an art than a science. Often development teams bite off more than they can chew... and some of that content will be spit back out. It is incredibly disheartening to see the dialog you wrote or the level you scripted cut after you've put in hundreds of hours of work on it.

Understand What You Enjoy

If you have weighed the personal costs of a career in game development and are still committed to pursuing it the next step is developing an understanding of *why* you want to build games. This might seem trivial or even silly but it is useful for a variety of reasons:

1.   **Job Interviews** You will be asked "why do you want to work in the games industry?" or, more specifically, "why do you want to work for us?".

2.   **Your Specialization** Understanding what you enjoy best about games helps you focus on developing skills in that area. Whether it be puzzle design, game audio, cinematics, graphics programming... whatever... play around with a variety of game development tools. What tasks do you enjoy doing? Which would you prefer to avoid? This will help you figure out what

your role in a company might be (in CHAPTER 2, I list some typical design positions).

What Do You Like?

To understand your likes and dislikes, it is worthwhile to think about some of the recent games you played, and maybe some more distant titles from your past.
If I were to do this exercise, I might write the following:

> *The games I enjoy are 'balanced' -- that is, they have story, exploration, rule system progression, and engaging combat. When a game focuses too much attention on one or two elements, at the expense of the others, I lose interest.*
>
> *I want fun, I want to be surprised; I love stumbling across something in a game I was not expecting. I remember an old adventure game from the 90s before games regularly had spoken (voice recorded) dialog and when my avatar walked into a bar there was a song playing with actual lyrics. That blew my mind. I enjoy games that have me exploring an expansive world that feels like it could be real. This does not mean that it has to be real (NPCs do not actually need jobs or day-night routines or things like that) but it does mean the designers should be careful not to purposefully destroy the illusion of reality. Having a day-night cycle (wherein the sun actually rises and sets) and having non-player characters (NPCS) standing around doing nothing destroys the illusion. In a game with no day night cycle I can handle them standing around, I just imagine that I'm always arriving to the area during the day when they would be standing there. It is about perspective.*

So I enjoy story and exploration and rules systems. Role-playing games (RPGs) tend to have a good mix of those three elements, which, not surprisingly is why they are one of my favorite styles of game to play. I also enjoy real time strategy games (RTSs) because they usually have reasonable exploration and strong rules system -- though rarely an engaging story.

Why Do You Want to Build?

I have always created content for others. It is what I do. I like building things with my imagination. I also like having an audience.
Developing videogames with BioWare was a dream come true. A lot of that was because I was creating product... a physical entity that could be seen on a store shelf by a customer and then picked up, carried to a counter and purchased. I loved walking

through the aisles with friends and pointing out the titles I had worked on. I did not do this to be arrogant... I did it because I was proud of the effort that had been poured into building the product and the sacrifices every member of the team had to make to build the best possible experience.

Think about that. Will building videogames make you proud? Will you be satisfied making games? When I joined BioWare I had a more significant salary offer on the table... a straight up programming job building virtual cogs in a massive software enterprise. There would have been customers but never a product. It was an easy decision for me. I wanted to build things that people wanted. I wanted to build a product.

Do you?

Once you understand what you like to play and why you want to build games of your own, start enhancing your game design skills.

Education

Before I continue I should make a note about education requirements. This will vary but I seldom see job postings asking for less than a Bachelors degree (back in the late 90s, when I was hired at BioWare the design posting I applied to required a Bachelors of Computing Science).

In a small startup hiring requirements are more flexible but once a company becomes relatively well known the bachelors degree becomes a mandatory requirement, even in fields such as design where there is not an official or stated education path. Think of the bachelors degree as a filter -- the exact degree did not generally matter, simply knowing that the potential employee was able to complete four years of college or university helps lighten a stack of applications. I am certain we missed quality designers but the truth is that BioWare seldom lacked for applicants. It is up to the aspiring designer to ensure that they give themselves the best chance at being looked at. I think you need a bachelors degree to have that chance now, in the industry.

> *Many specializations in game development require even higher levels of education, though this is more common in other departments such as programming where it was not uncommon to hire masters level or doctorate level employees for specialized tasks such as graphics programming or artificial intelligence.*

Take a look at job postings and see what they are asking for, in regards to the positions you covet. This will help guide your career preparation. Beyond just educational requirements see what additional materials applicants are being asked to submit. Supplying demos or mods (levels you have built for existing games) is a common requirement.

When I originally applied to BioWare they wanted technical skills and writing ability. So, along with my resume I sent several stories. One of these stories was later merged into an existing plot for Baldur's Gate 2!

I should make a quick comment about game design schools (these are dedicated facilities providing degrees focusing on game development). At one time I was actively against them. I thought they were too expensive and too specialized. I think the courses themselves have improved over time and my stance on them is more neutral. I still think, for the money being asked, that it makes more sense for a prospective designer to earn a degree in Computing Science... you will gain most of the skills you need to enter the industry *and* you have a more general purpose degree (which means you can support yourself while hunting down your desired game development career).

Teaching Yourself

No matter the educational path you have taken all designers need to enhance their skills. The best way to do this is to build games. And no, that does not mean you have to start your own game studio. The two best ways to hone your skills are to **mod**ify existing games and to build small games.

Modding and building games will require a personal computer. It is assumed you have one, even if you intend to develop games for consoles or mobile devices, the development platforms require a personal computer, and obviously, any career in game development requires knowledge of how to use a computer and the standard tools on them.

If you intend to work with a company that specializes in building apps for iPhones and iPads, you will have to buy a MacOS computer as the development environment for those devices requires it.

Modding

Find games that ship with toolsets and try building maps and short scenarios. In most cases the toolset is a version of the same tool that the designers who built the game used, although usually with fewer features. Learning how to use the toolset will help prepare you to use the kinds of tools you might use in your career.

I'm biased but I think the Neverwinter Nights toolset is the ideal game development learning platform. It allows you to build terrain, write dialog, and learn basic scripting (via a simplified programming language). There are many tutorials online for Neverwinter Nights and because you are exposed to all the major game development disciplines you receive a mini course in building a full game whenever you use it.

Building It Small

When you are ready to try to build a stand-alone game of your own, start small. I suggest trying to make a simple Flash or HTML5 game or an iPhone/iPad game.

It might seem daunting but there are numerous tutorials available online. I would suggest looking at those tutorials and learning how to modify the example code to achieve the results you want.

A year ago I messed around with Flash, not knowing anything about it and found a tutorial that walked me through the basics. (The 3rd part of the series is here: **Flash tutorial** http://www.emanueleferonato.com/2006/12/06/flash-game-creation-tutorial-part-3/). In Flash (using this and the other tutorials on that site) I did my own art and programming and created a multi-level word-hunting game for my kids. Not something I would show off but I learned the basic skills required to construct moderately complicated Flash games.

You might also look at books that delve into the experience in more detail, such as titles focused on iPhone game development. Check out Amazon and see what is available but for a beginner the tutorials are more than sufficient.

The key is to start small, adding bits of gameplay at a time. Get basic features working before introducing complications. I would generally start by adding movement, then boundaries (walls), then other features.

If you enjoy building your own game and think you have created a fun and engaging experience you might consider selling it on your own. While I encourage this you should be aware that there are many additional details to worry about (testing, translation, deployment, and such). Here books or discussions by experts who have done this on their own became even more useful. The links section at the end of this book has a few sites that may be of interest to you.

Some of these advanced topics will also be discussed in later books in the Lazy Designer series.

Learning Technical Skills

It does not matter what role you want to play for a game developer -- storyboard artist, animator, writer, or producer -- honing your technical skills makes you more valuable.

You, like most applicants I encountered, probably have the vision of a *dream position*. For most designers it was to be either the lead designer -- setting out the vision and assembling the major building blocks for the game being built -- or the lead writer who sculpts the game world and narrative. These are great goals to aspire towards and it is important to build skills leading towards them yet too many applicants are so focused on landing the dream position that they miss numerous other opportunities that would help **get their foot in the door**.

Want to be a storyboard artist? This is a prestigious position and it is tough to land that position, especially with an established developer but if the aspiring storyboard artist learned how to make icons and even better learned *tricks* to create them faster than anyone else that artist's value is going to increase.

They might not be able to start as a concept artist but getting hired is the first, not the final step, in their game industry career.

Likewise it is important for a designer, despite an intended specialization, to be well rounded. Having strong technical skills will allow a designer to be able to tackle new and unfamiliar tasks, thoroughly and efficiently.

- **Write Code** A design **scripter** has to take dialog, locations, creatures and make them all function together, generally through the use of a pseudo programming language known as a scripting language. So, knowing how to program is essential to scripters. In the art department there are technical artists who are experts at exporting and converting art data between various formats. In the quality testing department there are testers who write testing tools, build automated tests and so on. Every department benefits from having individuals who are capable at writing software.

- **Learn Excel** Being able to create a simple spreadsheet on demand is often useful, whether it is to organize the files you have to deliver by month's end, to build a mini-schedule for your sub department, or to track resource usage.

- **Database Designer** If you can, learn how to use simple databases. More powerful than spreadsheets, databases can be of significant benefit when storing gameplay data, user feedback, locations and status of art files. Databases allow the proficient user to export that data into any format that teammates or management might need. They can be used to automate documentation or reporting gameplay concerns.

- **Draw!** While not really a technical skill, being able to make simple sketches and drawings can help you communicate. Additionally, design documents benefit when the text is broken up with images so communicating visually is a worthwhile skill to enhance. If you, like me, have absolutely no drawing skill consider using sketching or flowcharting software, which will assist you in creating quality images.

> Over the years I worked at BioWare as a designer I learned how to build art models, automate Word documentation, create databases, PHP & MySQL coding, and advanced Excel trickery. I worked with numerous asset and bug tracking packages, and built prototype tools in a variety of programming languages. Being flexible and willing to learn new skills -- and demonstrating that you have done this previously, before the job interview -- helps nudge your potential employer into employing you.

Becoming a Writer

Because the game writer's career is the one aspect of game development that I'm asked to describe most often I will focus more attention on it here than I will other positions. For the non-writers among you some of the advice that follows, such as the suggestions for making contacts with existing game writers, apply to any other position you might be considering.

First, let me be clear: there is no secret trick to break into a game company as a writer. As I mentioned earlier being skilled at *other things* is vital. If you are hired you can prove your competence as a writer later. Few game companies hire writers. Many use freelance writers, under temporary contracts. The stable game writing career with benefits, free breakfasts, and a sports cars is a rare beast.

> *I do not know much about freelance game writing, as I have never done that nor have I worked with a freelance writer. I will focus my discussion on the staff writer, a position I am familiar with.*

The On-The-Staff Writer

This is a writer who is a standard employee of a videogame company with all the perks (and disadvantages) that entails. As I mentioned above there are few companies that offer this position... most writing in most companies is done by the system/level designers, or freelance writers.

BioWare is an exception. I do not know how many writers BioWare employs now but counting all of its studios I would guess that they employ about twenty full-time writers. I'm biased but I still think this is the best studio for a video game writer to try to write for. Haunting **their job openings page** (http://www.bioware.com/careers) is your best bet to keep an eye out for writing positions.

At BioWare several of the early writers, the ones I worked with on Baldur's Gate 2, Neverwinter Nights, Jade Empire, and Dragon Age, came with backgrounds in writing for role-playing games. Others had published short stories or novels. There is no single key to why some writers stayed with the company and others left. Writing non-linear narrative is demanding and even experienced novelists struggled with changing their writing style to handle all the various ways that a player, who has control over the story, can thwart their story-telling attempts.

Basically storytellers who could adapt their writing to meet the demands of non-linear narrative thrived at BioWare.

> *I should also mention that the writers at BioWare, while considered full-time writers, also performed other design tasks but I think most of them, now, primarily design levels and write.*

Other Writing Opportunities

Scan the Credits

One way to find game writing jobs is to scan the credits of games that have decent stories and see who is credited as writer. If there's more than one writer it is likely that the company has at least some writers on staff. After getting a couple names google them and see if you can find out more about them! Yes that's stalking, but it is all in a good cause -- getting you a job. If the writer appears to be actually working at a particular company (instead of freelancing) learn more about the company, the games they make, and whether they are hiring or not.

> *Keep in mind that a first-person shooter studio has little need for writers compared with an ambitious 200 hour role-playing game with eight hundred thousand words of dialog.*

For example, these are the writing credits for Dragon Age: Origins (taken from **MobyGames** http://www.mobygames.com/game/windows/dragon-age-origins/credits)

Lead Writer
David Gaider
Writers

Ferret Baudoin, Sheryl Chee, Daniel Erickson, Jennifer Brandes Hepler, Mary Kirby, Lukas Kristjanson, Jay Turner

Credit surfing might not be an overly productive method of determining writers in a company because many companies do not seem to label writers as such. I assumed Bethesda (Fallout 3, Oblivion) and Obsidian had on-staff writers but I did not see writers mentioned in the credits! This is likely because the game designers do the writing in addition to the game design at those companies.

Research Conventions

There are several video game conventions. Do not bother attending them unless you can afford to but do scan their events. Look for panels concerning Storytelling or Writing and find out the names of the presenters. Figure out the games they worked on and check their websites. Maybe even toss an e-mail or two their way and ask about their careers; you'll probably find a willing correspondent. I officially give you permission to contact any writer in the industry.

This is the link to the **schedule for the Game Developer's Conference**: http://www.gdconf.com/. Also look for fiction, comic or role-playing game conventions, they will occasionally bring in guest speakers from the video game industry. Follow one around and pester them with questions.

Forums -- Become Part of the Community

Visit video game forums and start interacting with the developers there. Learn to differentiate the various design positions and build relationships. It can help you down the road and following the discussions will give you a better idea of who does what.

Write Your Own!

Anybody considering writing dialog for video games needs to play around with the existing tools (such as the Neverwinter Nights/Dragon Age dialog editors) and examine how dialog is constructed.

Got Something Else To Offer?

Again, I want to reiterate that if you would like to write, or be involved in the story creation on a video game consider getting your foot in the door in another position. A reasonable foot-in-the-door might be as a technical designer/scripter. Take on additional writing tasks when they present themselves and you'll find yourself doing more writing down the road. If not just sneak text into the game... the managers love that.

Expect the road to a career in game development to be a rocky one. Once you have mastered the skills you need and have narrowed down your list of potential companies to work for you will have to go about the actual nuts and bolts of applying for the job.

The Job Search

The Resume

Do not inflate your resume. Do not exaggerate your past duties. I should not have to say that, but here I am, saying it. Be honest but descriptive. What skills would you bring to the company? If you are relatively inexperienced being good at a variety of tasks will increase your chances of being hired.

The Cover Letter

You can find lots of general advice online about how to compose a cover letter. Here is some specific advice in regards to what I liked to see:

- **You Play Games** Should be clear that you are a gamer and better yet, that you've played the games this developer has made. Specific examples work better than "I've played games since I was two. Used to drive my mom nuts."
- **Focus on skills** What do you bring to the company and what do you value about what the company does: "I am an accomplished writer but desire to improve my understanding of non-linear story design and your company seems to be kicking butt at that."
- **Get your terminology right** Look at job postings online to see what they call the various specialties. Calling yourself a writer might be better than saying "word monkey", for example.
- **This is not a chat line** Avoid using writing shortcuts that you might use when posting an update to your Facebook status. Use proper writing. Does not have to be an essay but it should be somewhat formal. No emoticons.
- **Do not make it obvious you are only using them** You might think that working for Developer XYZ is a great stepping stone for your career. Do not say that. No one wants to think of themselves as a stepping stone.
- **Do not beg** Do not beg for the job. Do not talk about your sick kitten.
- **Do not be arrogant** Do not go overboard on the other extreme and make it seem as if that developer is going to go bankrupt if they do not hire you. Telling a potential employer that "only an idiot would pass up the chance to hire me" is probably a bad idea. Just saying.

Some of my examples above might seem silly but when hiring for BioWare I saw all of the above at one time or another.

The Portfolio

Most design positions will ask (or should ask) for a demo of some kind. Basically a game or a mod. Look at their job posting and see what they are asking for and when possible build a game in the tools they want you to.

The lighter your resume the better your portfolio should be -- a writer should have great writing samples, a technical designer should have games or mods of existing games. Even if they do not ask for a game demo consider submitting one to them once you are at the phone interview phase of the process (especially if you feel you have built something compelling). I hired many designers based on seeing what they were able to create, not because of what they wrote in their resume or said in the interview.

At BioWare we used to ask for submission of adventures built using the Neverwinter Nights toolset. Occasionally we received submissions built with other platforms... when possible we viewed these but if we did not have easy access to them it would take us longer to review them.

Applying

Use the appropriate application process as outlined on the company's website. Blind e-mailing a generic cover letter/portfolio to 10000 companies will result in 9999 complete ignores (I would like to think at least one company would give a reply of some sort).

The Interview

Interviews, whether by phone or in person, can be nerve wracking (both for the interviewee and the interviewer!) Again, instead of being general, I'll be specific about what I liked to see when hiring.

- **Engaged** Do not dominate the conversation, it is for the interviewer to lead it, but do try to ask your own questions. Get clarifications on what the position would entail.
- **Answer the Question** Do not dodge an uncomfortable question. I would rather an honest answer of "no, I have no experience with that" especially if followed up with "but I have learned and excelled at using something similar. I'm sure I could pick it up."

- **What do you hate?** I alway asked interviewees to dissect a level in an existing title and explain how it could be improved. This is a good question to prepare for.
- **Again, Don't be Arrogant** When answering a question about what you might improve in an existing game, do not insult the designers who worked on the title. They might be the ones interviewing you. But you should give an honest criticism.

Another question to prepare for, which I have had asked of me during interviews and which I asked myself on many occasions is "What mistake did you make on the job?" This is a hard question to answer because nobody wants to admit to making mistakes. But admitting to the mistake and maybe illuminating how you had learned from the mistake is important.

Here's the answer I would give.

One of my faults as a designer was that I did not embrace the concept of digital distribution (selling software over the Web, instead of in a retail package) readily enough. Why I was not that interested in selling games, or game add-ons, digitally has much to do with my earlier discussion about wanting to build product... a physical thing that customers could purchase.

This was not because I did not understand the appeal of being able to purchase and download software digitally. It was because digital distribution did not appeal to me as a creator! I wanted to create a product. Even though for some it seems bizarre to think of software as a physical entity, it was, when I started in the industry. It had a box and sometimes even maps and other goodies inside it. So I was reluctant to push for digital distribution.

I was in a position with a fair deal of influence on others and my lack of interest in digital distribution probably had some effect on others. Had I been more positively favored towards it, earlier incorporation of digital distribution features probably would have occurred on some titles.

My reluctance was a mistake. I needed to reevaluate what I considered a product... a game does not need a box and a cloth map to be a product. The product is not diminished by lacking physicality. It is even enhanced, especially if the potential audience grows larger.

As a writer I love physical books. There are magazines I want to see my stories appear in. I want to be able to point those magazines out to friends when I am in a store. When my novels are published I want to do the same thing.

But my experience with digital distribution has taught me to examine where traditional publishing is heading. By the time I have a publishing contract... will there be bookstores? Or only the 'big name authors' carving out space in the Walmarts and such of the world? My friends and family seem more excited now when I tell them a story reprint of mine is able to be downloaded onto the Kindle or Sony Reader or Kobo. They are less excited by the prospect of a print magazine sale that is difficult for them to obtain.

So, as a writer, I had to strongly contemplate publishing electronically, to reach the audience I wanted and to have the control I wanted over my work.

What Not To Do

I will end this chapter with a caveat. Earlier I suggested contacting an expert in the field you want to become a part of. Keep in mind that just because a designer out there is willing to pass some advice to you does not mean that you should send them your unfinished storyline ideas, game design documents, or other material.

This has happened to me several times and it always creates an uncomfortable situation. I cannot read other people's work or help them publish it. I do not have the time and I do not want to be involved in a legal dispute later (i.e., if someone feels I stole their idea). So, please do not do this to anybody else!

Here's a bit more of an elaboration.

Who Makes a Game?

Games are created by dozens, if not hundreds of people. Freelance writers are hired by some companies to write game scripts but usually only after having proven themselves, either in the game industry or in movies or television or books... even these writers would generally be fleshing out someone else's vision. Not their own. Even after years with BioWare it would have been incredibly unlikely for me to be able to make *my game*. While I could influence the direction of games being made the higher level design constraints were set in place by employees above me.

If you truly feel you have the next great game idea your best option would be to found your own gaming company (or join a relatively new company).

Here's a list of other suggestions that might help you realize your vision:

- **Form a squad** Join a gaming community, either one near you or one online. Meet with like-minded developers. You might find people who are willing to volunteer their time to help you build your game, especially if you have skills that you can offer in exchange.

- **Publish it** Try publishing your game script idea as a novella (look at **www.duotrope.com** and other writing market sites for places to sell stories).

- **Start 'er up** Look for a new gaming developer that is actively hiring, especially if you have other skills that might get your foot in the door. Once you've worked for them a bit start talking about your script... if they are a really new company and floundering to create that first great project your script might be what they need. (Probably best not to mention your script in the interview unless you have managed to have it published elsewhere first.)

- **How about a movie?** There are creative enthusiasts out there who make short movies using game animation tools. You will not make any money from this but it might be satisfying to collaborate with someone and see your script turned into real animation. Do a search for **machinima** and you'll turn up plenty of information.

Summary

I realize that some of this is discouraging. The path to videogame developer stardom is tangled and at times difficult to traverse. I was discouraged starting out. As a veteran of the industry though I can say it was worth it.

I started work with BioWare in August 1999. My first day was especially memorable since it never happened.

I was all nervous and excited and took my hour long commute across the city (never had a vehicle back then) to get to work and…

…it was closed. See, August in Alberta, Canada gives us a nice little holiday and that happened to coincide with my first day of work. The doors were all locked up, I had no way to get in. I had a couple initial thoughts.

Maybe they had not actually hired me. It was a joke and everyone was behind those locked doors, big smiles on their faces. Or maybe BioWare had shut down. After all they had only put out two games to this point (Baldur's Gate and Shattered Steel). Maybe they were now out of business and all the smiles and handshaking during the interview had been the employees putting on brave faces aboard a sinking ship.

In either case I was kicking myself for declining a higher paying programming position with another software company. Using a pay phone (yes, those used to exist at one time) I called the office.

Ring. Ring. Ring.

Finally, an answer. It was the art director of an unannounced project -- Neverwinter Nights -- and he told me nobody else was at work, to go home, and to come back the next day.

So I did.

CHAPTER 2 - Being Better

> Being a designer is the best job in the world. Designers bring the fun, and what could be better than that?

Congratulations! You got the job.

Now get to work!

Getting hired is merely the first step. How your career develops will largely be dictated by your performance. There will be factors outside your control -- such as projects being canceled -- but for the most part your ability to complete tasks to quality, communicate effectively with your superiors and your peers in other departments, and to be accurate and honest with your progress, will be the measure of your career in making videogames.

I will start with a discussion of what you might expect in your work environment and then explain how you can improve your on the job performance. The final section of this chapter will address how to test your game, deliver feedback and receive feedback.

Obviously, each potential game development position will have varying expectations but these sections should supply you with general guidelines to assist you in constructing the career you want.

What to Expect

Training

In all likelihood you will receive some training before actually assuming any responsibilities. The extent of the training will vary on the maturity of the company, the size of the team, what current deadlines the team is under, and whether there is anybody around to do the actual training.

At its best training will include one-on-one time with an experienced designer, going over the tools and being shown examples of what your day to day duties will be, how task tracking systems work, and the general procedures and operation of the company. You will have time, under guidance, to acquaint yourself with the tools and will likely develop some throwaway content to develop your skills.

That would be an ideal and fertile training ground. More likely, you will be placed in front of a computer in a crowded office (or worse, in a closet by yourself) and given a task list.

No matter the quality of your training you will only get out of it what you put into it.

If training consists of being thrown at the tools and told to play for a couple days with no additional feedback, then do your best. Talk to other developers, (even if only on their lunch break because they are too busy otherwise). Figure out the tips and tricks. Hunt the company's intranet for a tutorial... has another employee recorded video of aspects of the development process relevant to you? Is there an internal wiki? Try to dig up project specific documentation too -- relevant design documents, vision documents, marketing documents? This acquaints you with the project and its direction; useful information for when you start tackling tasks.

As well, write down what you learn and post it to an appropriate place in the company's documentation system. If you have created something useful let the relevant folks know (human resources department and management). They may not have realized that there is a void in their training process and some constructive nudging could lead towards a better training process.

Eventually you will migrate out of training and into actual game development. In the next section I'll take a look at some of the various positions available in the design department and their responsibilities.

Positions

There is minimal standardization in the game development industry, in regards to positions, so please understand that the following descriptions will not match perfectly with the positions available at all companies.

Management

Director of Design - At BioWare there were two chains of command for any employee: a game project chain (with a project director overseeing content leads) and a department chain with each department having their own director. The Director of Design was responsible for hiring, skill improvement, allocating people to projects and resolving human resources *issues* arising on projects that could not be resolved at the project level. At various times there was also an assistant design director. All designers, including design leads, had to report to the design director.

Lead Designer/Creative Director - This designer was in charge of a full game with responsibilities that included managing the staff, acquiring (through the design department chain) additional staff, training, designing the game with the rest of the team, and high level creation and management of design documents.

Specializations

Each design specialization generally had their own lead (i.e., a Lead Writer, a Lead Cinematic Designer, et cetera) who was responsible for day to day management of that design subset as well as driving the design vision for that subset. These managers would report to the Lead Designer.

WRITER

Primarily the writers at BioWare wrote dialog -- the lines each character in their areas of responsibility spoke. Writers also created soundsets (the non-dialog utterances of characters, such as battle grunts and ambient chatter), item descriptions, journal descriptions, follower dialog, and menu help text.

Writers often planned/designed their gameplay levels and wrote documentation for those levels (usually in tandem with a technical/level designer). It was often the case however that writer might not plan all the levels they ended up writing dialog for. When project scope changed writers could be assigned to levels planned by another team member. So, generally the writer had full design ownership of their areas of responsibility but not always.

EDITORS

On earlier projects writers had edited their own writing but to meet scheduling and quality demands editors became necessary. Editors were responsible for making sure that naming patterns and style rules are enforced. As well, depending on the project, they helped shorten individual sentences or suggested places for words to be cut to meet word count budgets.

TECHNICAL DESIGNERS

Technical designers (often just referred to as game designers) had several specializations, including data entry (i.e., filling in 'stats' for creatures), rule system design and scripting.

Data entry involved tasks such as placing creatures in levels, filling in data tables or assigning statistics to creatures. A rules system designer (sometimes its own specialization) designed the rules systems, games progression and special powers and worked with programming to implement these. As well a system designer often worked with the art and programming teams to design user interfaces.

Scripting was the process by which creature resources (dialog, art, animation, sound) were put into an art level and made to come to life. The exact process varied by project but involved setting logic variables in dialog as well as generating behaviors for creatures -- making them talk or walk or fight. Scripting was light-weight programming that transformed static resources into the artificial reality that players explored.

While technical designers seldom designed gameplay levels senior technical designers generally assisted whomever was designing the levels (generally the writers) to help ensure that the plots being conceived could be implemented. Technical designers also spent significant of time play testing both their own work and that of their team mates.

CINEMATIC DESIGNERS

In early BioWare games most (if not all) cinematics were created by animators, artists and sound engineers. However it became clear that the narrative demands of story-rich games required creating more cinematics (and to make dialog more cinematic). At the same time we needed to avoid raising development costs too drastically. One way to do this was to have technical designers build small cinematic scenes in-engine (basically these designers created scripts, like they would for combat, but with the intention that they were showing interaction between game characters on the screen... effectively scripting in-game *plays* for the player to watch).

Most of these early cinematics were done using only repurposed animation and sound resources but as the games became more sophisticated cinematic design became a sub department within design and had access to its own tools and other resources.

> When I started with BioWare there were only three kinds of designers - writers, management, and 'other designers'. There was overlap between the positions (i.e., management was writing and scripting, writers were scripting, and scripters were sometimes writing). Over time as the games became more complicated the other specializations were created. This was a general theme across all departments.

Work Environment

So, what is it like to work in a game development studio? Free food? Recreation rooms? Flexible vacations?

Sure.

It is likely that any game design studio you work for will have those perks. It is also likely that they will be informal, in regards to dress code and conduct. Still the actual social dynamics of game development will deviate greatly from studio to studio and from team to team.

Small Team, Big Team

Team size will vary depending on the company and the project. In the early days of BioWare the teams were relatively small. Smaller teams, I found, tended to allow the individual designer more freedom and control over what they were working on. As the team size increased more management procedures were erected to help control the content that entered the game. These controls helped to keep the team committed to the vision (vision on smaller teams is more easily enforced through direct interaction between management and staff; something that becomes less achievable as team size increases) but at times these procedures can dampen creativity and employee ownership over their work.

On my first few titles, after the game shipped, I often discovered content in games I worked on that I had known nothing about during development - the writers, designers and artists had just put the content in because they thought players would enjoy it. Spontaneous design is often discouraged in larger studios out of worry over inappropriate material being inserted without management's approval. (These worries are not entirely unfounded -- there *has* been inappropriate content hidden in games).

More freedom is generally given to individual designers in a small company because there is a lack of time/ability/resources for the leads to plan for *everything*. Some design work might be spur of the moment -- a level has turned out to be larger than planned due to a miscommunication and now a designer has to scramble to create content to put into it, for example. In a more developed company, procedures to make game development more efficient might actually remove the need for individual designers to contribute as much. Fewer miscommunications might create fewer design opportunities!

Finally, the nature of the intellectual property (IP) being worked on influences how easy it is to add content:

> When working on Baldur's Gate 2 we had a master item list but it was possible for any designer to create a magical item and basically insert it (generally, but not always, with some approval from the manager). This process worked reasonably well because Baldur's Gate 2 was based on the Dungeons and Dragons (D&D) license; most designers understood D&D well and knew how to construct a properly balanced item for that game system.
>
> While developing Dragon Age: Origins a more technical approach to building and maintaining the master item list was created. This was done mostly because this

was a new rules system and no designer truly understood how it all worked (unlike a Dungeons and Dragons title). Individual designers were unable to tweak items to the same extent as they could have an item from Baldur's Gate 2, whereas a manager, by modifying some data tables, could make sweeping changes to balance with a few tweaks. Something that could not have been done on the D&D title.

On the other hand, when working with your own IP, there are several benefits that do override the negatives of working with an unfamiliar rule system and game world. During the planning phase of Dragon Age: Origins, for example, designers were free to dream up anything they wanted for the item system. We would not have had this enhanced creative ownership when working within the framework of an existing IP.

The scope and scheduling of a game also has an influence on the work environment. In my first five years at BioWare I shipped several titles; in my last five only one. The games were larger and more complicated to make and thus, they took longer to produce.

As a designer I found this unsatisfying.

The player's reaction to the game is the feedback that I, as a designer craved. Additionally when a game is developed over a long period of time the team has to constantly modify content that has already been created.

For example... a competitors title might be released while you are still building your game and if it looks substantially better your team might be compelled to redo the game's art. This in turn could introduce another delay in the production schedule! Basically once you start working on multi-year titles what happens in the outside world has a greater chance of delaying your game further and even affecting the content you put into the game.

Hours

There is unpaid overtime in the videogames industry. When I was enjoying the work I did not care... it was a blast working away with an engaged team on new content and dreaming up ways to entertain the player. But when responsibilities increased and schedules tightened the job itself did become more stressful.

Competition for Success

I know some newcomers to the industry worry about promoting themselves in order to receive desired promotions. In my experience if competent employees proved themselves they were rewarded. There was no cutthroat atmosphere. I recommend working hard, improving your skills, communicating effectively and doing your best to help and mentor others. Maybe you will not receive all the rewards you feel you should but you will enjoy the job more. Which is probably more important in the long-term.

Task Management

Overview

A few weeks into my job with BioWare I found myself overwhelmed. The tasks kept piling on. I had only ever received a few dozen e-mails in my entire life and now that was how many I was receiving every day.

Most of them were asking me to do more work!

To keep up I developed some task management systems for myself that worked more or less for my career, albeit requiring the occasional modification along the way to keep up with changing technology.

Here's a short discussion on what worked (and an example of what did not).

Get Lazy

One quick way to accomplish more is to improve the work process itself. If you have repetitious tasks that take significant time to complete determine methods to complete the task more quickly, even if it means expending effort to build tools (batch files or small utility programs) to do so. A small expenditure of time up front saves loads of time on the actual task.

Convert tasks you receive into prioritized checklists. This makes it easy to know which tasks are complete and which are not when asked. This might seem obvious but many struggling newcomers do not do this... they assume they'll remember the tasks given to them and become overwhelmed as more duties are added to them.

Technical Skills

In CHAPTER 1 I discussed why technical skills were important. The previous section is an example of why. Because I had the ability to program a quick and dirty scripting editor I was able to improve my task completion time. This made me more valuable to the team.

There's no right or wrong programming language to program in. The important thing is to learn *one*. Once you do that, adapting to new programming languages is not difficult. And if you are only developing temporary tools for yourself, the language you use is generally not relevant (as long as it works on your work computer).

Learning a programming language also helps you to think logically -- learning how to break complex tasks into simpler *stepping stones* is a valuable skill that will serve you well in every facet of game development. I am far from a skilled programmer but I learned how to enjoy writing code and often I still finding myself creating utilities to give myself a break from more stressful tasks. So, for me, programming serves two purposes -- it is my method of relaxing and it helps reduce future stress because I create tools to reduce my workload.

Estimates

I eventually learned to **under-promise** and **over-deliver**. This was probably my most effective task management strategy. Not only did it look impressive (I always completed more than I said I would and I did it faster than I said) but it also taught me to estimate -- because I was not completely overwhelmed I could assess how long I had predicated the task would take and record this information. Eventually I had enough data that I could hone my estimates better and be more accurate when estimating future tasks.

My estimates improved (though I always continued to under-promise/over-deliver). I was able to build schedules and see my entire task load in a global view. I realized I had time to finish all my tasks. Gradually my stress reduced (at least until I became a lead designer).

> *While following this philosophy gives you the appearance of being a diligent worker you still have to complete a reasonable amount of tasks! I could not have gotten away with small workloads and huge timelines. You have to be realistically realistic.*

Don't Deliver Low Quality Work

In an effort to meet your schedules you might finish the bare bones of a task, honoring it to the letter of the request but not to the spirit. Do not do this. Do not finish a task and say to your manager, "I think this sucks but maybe you might kinda sort of tolerate it, no?"

I've read interviews with editors for short story magazines and some say they receive this kind of apology in cover letters accompanying story submissions occasionally (and I saw it occasionally as a design manager). If you are not confident in what you have written/designed you need to improve it before you show anybody else!

If you honestly do not know whether it is good or not then say so but as a designer you really should *know* -- at least the difference between terrible and great. The line between okay and not-okay might be harder to differentiate until you are more experienced.

> *On the other hand if you think you have created something amazing but say it sucks to mess with your manager's expectations, well, you are just being weird.*

So: do not promise too much and kill yourself trying to be a task completion hero. But do not undersell your skills either.

Single-Tasking

You will always have dozens of simultaneous tasks.

Do not work on them all at the same time! Complete a task and only then move to others. Multi-tasking is a lie. You cannot work efficiently on more than one task at a time. In many of my performance reviews I am praised for multi-tasking. That was an illusion. I worked on one task and completed it and then moved to the next. When I tried to actually multi-task, I failed.

> *One exception would be if you are blocked on your current task (i.e, perhaps waiting for an e-mail reply to a question you sent to your manager asking to clarify requirements). When you are blocked it does make sense to move to another task.*

Test Cycle

I am a obsessive tester of my own work. This was especially useful in the learning phase on a project. Instead of spending hours implementing content before testing it I would instead implement a few details at a time, push that content into the game engine and test. This implementation-test cycle hones a designer's skill and minimizes distraction and stress. It is easier to solve one problem at a time (i.e., why did this door not unlock) as opposed to a collection of issues (nothing in the level works!)

If the game engine you are using does not support such rapid implementation and testing then get the programmers to improve the engine. Seriously! Enabling rapid iteration saves money and improves quality.

Purge Thy E-mail

I made sure that I answered all my e-mail every day (I tried to continue this process even when I started getting a hundred or more e-mails a day, never quite succeeded but I was always as prompt as possible in delivering replies). I categorized my e-mail| and tried to reply to everything even if my reply was no more than a quick _okay, got it_.

If the e-mail was a task I copied it to my task checklist and moved the e-mail to a *deal with later* folder so that I could remember to reply to the person when the task was completed.

> *By moving an e-mail right away out of your inbox you help reduce the time you spend re-reading messages that you have already dealt with.*

Folders are an Unnecessary Evil

If your e-mail software has a categorization or color-coding system, use that instead of using folders. Flag the e-mail as it comes in according to a handful of categories.

Basically I assigned mail to one of three categories -- **Do Immediately, 'Do Soon, Look at Eventually**. I also had other minor categories such as Dragon Age, Mass Effect and so on to label what project the e-mail was about -- the neat thing, and the advantage over folders, is that you can assign more than one category to an e-mail; I could assign e-mail to two categories, such as *Do Soon | Dragon Age*.

On the discipline side of things -- and you need to have some discipline to be an effective game developer -- I tried to ensure that the 'do immediately' category was cleared daily. Was not always possible but it was a goal to strive towards.

> *Disclaimer. I don't entirely hate folders. In all fairness, they do have some usages and I would never completely ditch them. Basically color-coding/ categories only works wells if you have a limited number of categories. So I still have a folder in my inbox for each story I've written and then inside that folder I have all the e-mail acceptances/ rejections for that story. I could use a category system but as I have had over a hundred stories in circulation that would be a significant number of categories (and would make the category list cumbersome).*

What Did Not Work

Years ago I wrote my own task management software. While this was helpful for honing my estimates and automating a chunk of my task management it had flaws, the biggest of which was that I could not easily share the data with others. If your company does not have a task management tool it is best to use something simple like Excel because it is easily modified to work with a variety of systems and co-workers should know how to use it (and have access to it on their machines).

Random Bits

Designers are the last line of defense; if something goes wrong, and a designer can fix it and no one else will, then a designer should.

Here's a couple tips that will help increase your value to the company (and probably your satisfaction with the job).

In general these tips revolve around the idea of turning yourself into the go-to-designer -- somebody who other team members seek out when they need information and help.

- **Test Everything** Test (and send feedback) on every part of the game, especially those outside your area of responsibility. This allows you to understand how the entire game *fits* together and it hones your ability to give feedback (some suggestions on how to provide feedback are given later in this chapter). If you run out of things to test on your project, test another project in the company!

- **Become an Expert** Knowing a little bit about everything enables you to assist in a variety of roles but becoming an expert at *everything* is impossible. If you can master a specialization you should. Generally look at current holes in the project or company (things that are not going smoothly) and that you have an interest in learning more about. This can be as broad as being the 'cinematics guru' or narrowed down to specifics like mastering the certification requirements required to ship a title on the XBOX 360.

- **An Open Door Policy** Be available. Keep your office door open. Circulate on your free time to talk to your co-workers (but try not to disrupt them). Scan buglists and offer feedback... maybe you see a bug on somebody else's list and know how to fix it.

Giving and Receiving... Feedback

How to Submit Feedback that Will Make it into the Game and not the Recycling Bin

Feedback (re: bug reports, user analysis, critiques) is essential for many creative endeavors, from writing stories to making movies to designing games. Even the most talented game designer benefits from seeing their game through the eyes of a potential consumer. The only way to do that is to play the game.

Additionally knowing how to provide great feedback is essential for a designer and will prepare you for when you must solicit feedback and respond to it. Feedback in this section refers to *subjective* analysis of gameplay, interface, story, et cetera.

Consider this example:

Your interface sucks more than an vacuum cleaner. It's stupid and clunky. I hate it.

At best this feedback would become a data-point on a spreadsheet under the column of *did not like*. Most likely it would be simply deleted.

Why?

There's no information beyond 'did not like'. I don't care how clever an analogy the tester has constructed, or how intensely the tester disliked a feature, if they are not providing constructive feedback they are wasting the designer's time, and worse, company money.

An aside. My first edit of the above paragraph started with 'Because it's useless.' Often I have the tendency when providing feedback to be sarcastic or snarky. I (almost) always edit my bug reports to remove such negative bits.

What is constructive feedback? A websearch will provide several definitions, but at its core, constructive feedback should be:

- **Respectful** The moment the designer is put on the defensive they are going to stop listening. Being respectful keeps the door open between tester and designer. This includes being polite and avoiding 'hate' words, as well as explaining what did work -- quality testers do not assume that the designers know which features are fun. Occasionally a great feature is cut because nobody has mentioned they love it!
- **Detailed** List the elements under consideration, explaining what did not work and WHY.
- **Comparative** Is there a similar feature in another game that works better? Explain. Provide screenshots of the other game and/or supporting documentation.

- **Progressive** Suggest ways to improve the feature. Do not be offended if those suggestions are not taken; do follow up if no improvements are implemented.

So, an example of better feedback might be:

> *The main interface is a little cluttered. I love the variety of features available but a cleaner presentation would have allowed me to enjoy the game more.*
>
> *I've noticed that you are using a quick bar like GameXYZ. In that game they allow you to stretch the quick bar to any size. I suggest we adopt this approach, if possible. Start with a small quick bar and then allow the user to grow it as required, let them control the introduction of complexity when they are ready. See attached screenshots for an example of their quick bar in action.*

A tester, whether one in quality assurance or a designer providing feedback on another designer's levels, should never be arrogant or condescending. Feedback is an opportunity to help improve the overall product. And it is essential.

Be a good tester, with respectful and useful bug reports. Create an example that will serve as a roadmap in regards to how you expect your own content to be tested and reported on in the future.

> *In a later book I will explore some tools and debugging features that will assist with the testing process.*

Game Review Example

Another useful exercise is to write a game review for a in-progress title you are working on. As an example this is a review I posted of a BioWare title I did not work on but did playtest a little.

Review: Sonic Chronicles

If you haven't played **Sonic Chronicles** (http://en.wikipedia.org/wiki/Sonic_Chronicles:_The_Dark_Brotherhood) yet, I encourage you to give it a try.

Disclaimer #1 - I was not involved with the development of Sonic Chronicles.

Disclaimer #2 - I'm not a fan of the Sonic IP at all, so I'm addressing the game as a game, not part of the *sonic universe*.

This game is fun and there's little like it on the **Nintendo DS**. You get to explore beautifully drawn backgrounds, collecting items and companions. The story is quirky, interesting and well written. The target audience is for children and the game does a great job of catering to that audience, but I think there's enough depth for older players.

The Story

I'm not yet finished this... I have to fight for control of the DS with my wife and kids but I'm enjoying the story. The dialog is streamlined but still allows for some flexibility (and humor!) in the conversation choices. While some will find the story/conversation too simple (especially when compared with more mature titles) I think it works well considering that its a DS game.

The Combat System

I enjoyed the turn based combat, its fun and though simple, I feel I am making valid (and important) decisions in battle. I know I'm showing my age but what I do dislike about it is the action system, where I have to press points flashing across the screen quickly. I'm not very good at that.

I really like it that if I am defeated in battle I have to reload a save and come back to it. The combat is difficult enough that you will lose and need to retry with different tactics. This tactical decision making is important and creates *satisfying* combat.

Overall

Sonic Chronicles is definitely a solid game to add to your library of DS titles. The review scores might be low, but many of them were written by BioWare fans who wanted a more mature title and not the kid's game that Sonic was designed to be. There's expectations for BioWare to make a certain game and while Sonic has some BioWare elements (strong gameplay, choice-based dialog, engaging story) it should not to be compared with Baldur's Gate, Knights of the Old Republic, or Mass Effect. Apples and orange, eh?

Had this title been developed by another developer, it would have scored higher.

Don't Wait for Feedback, Ask for it

As a designer, feedback is the tool you use to navigate through the game design process. Sometimes outside opinion is mandated (your superiors certainly have expectations in regards to the game they are paying you to make) but you also should spread your net wider. Here's some suggestions on how to receive and use feedback.

Automate it when possible

Most feedback will be subjective (user opinion) but when putting that subjective feedback into context it is useful to have more automated data to compare it against. In a later book I'll dive into methods of using automated systems to track data (player movement and activity) but a brief mention of it here is warranted. Place hooks in the engine to output data points on activity you care about. If you have been given feedback that a particular area is boring take a look at a generated map that shows tester movements across that area. You might realize that everybody is missing the interesting encounters because there's a way to do a straight line path that avoids them! Tracking even such a simple activity as player movement is incredibly useful.

Make it Easy to Provide Feedback

Do not leave a feedback void... give testers and management a forum to provide feedback to you in the way that you want (and need and can use). Set up a poll (even better setup a poll/questionnaire at particular points in the game and tie this to the data you are already tracking about their play sessions). Submit company/project-wide polls on art/plot/dialog... whenever possible ensuring that the feedback is based on in-game play.

> *I found less value polling the company on out of game things like concept art. Better to have responses influenced by actual gameplay.*

Speak to the quality assurance testers (maybe even take them out to lunch) and ask them questions. Direct their focus. Maybe their answers will surprise you and make you realize that you need to be focusing your attention on other areas of your project.

You Can't Get Rid of (all) Opinions

What happens when you have received subjective feedback and it is from someone who can overrule your decisions? And what if the feedback is terrible?
How do you deal with that?
If possible I would sit the person down and have a discussion about *opinion* versus *data*. I would explain that while I value their opinion we need to compare their subjective feelings against objective data to make the right decision for the game. I would politely suggest that we restructure their feedback into a series of well structured poll questions and that we playtest the game and see if others have had similar problems. Then we would have a meeting to discuss all the collected feedback.

Handling Subjective Feedback

Learning how to incorporate subjective feedback is tricky so I'll lean on an example from the world of fiction writing to help explain the process.

Even successful authors use draft readers to help them judge whether their next novel is good. They do not rely on only one opinion... they have a team of readers. If the consensus is that the novel is weak (but the feedback varies), they know they have general problems in the text. If every reader picks up on the same issue as being problematic then the writer knows that they have a more specific issue to address. But the writer also realizes that his or her readers should not be the ones to suggest a solution to the problem. They have identified a problem (thank you!) and now it is time for the writer, or in our case, the game designer, to brainstorm ways to solve it.

> *This is not to say that those providing the feedback do not have the correct solution, it is just that sometimes it is too easy for the designer to jump on the offered solution without examining the problem in more detail first. The solution might work but the problem itself might be systemic of other issues, all of which could be dealt with by utilizing a completely different solution.*

Once you have a list of definite problems and potential solutions head out for lunch and do some brainstorming with your peers. Solicit their advice. Then think about it. Draft a plan, pass the plan around, slowly widening the feedback circle on it until you are certain you have solved the core issue.

> *If you have a situation where you are constantly changing features to suit the whims of upper management and you do not respect the decisions upper management makes there is only one solution.*
>
> *Start looking for a job at another studio.*
>
> *The gaming industry can be fun but if management becomes entrenched and is not open to logic or reason, go elsewhere.*

Summary

Learning the ropes and integrating yourself with the company culture are vital. The first few weeks are always a challenging mix of excitement and stress as you evaluate yourself and how you are fitting in with your new employer. The learning (hopefully) never stops and the skills you acquire will assist you in overcoming future obstacles.

I received my first and only negative employee review during my first few months working on Baldur's Gate 2. The basic gist was that I was not getting things done fast enough. Well, that frustrated me, so I really thought about why my performance was suffering.

At that time BioWare used the Infinity Scripting Language, and while the language itself was interesting, the method for using it was inefficient. All the coding for the design logic in the game was being written in notepad, or whatever other text editor a particular designer had access to. Then it was compiled via a command-line interface. Finding errors was complicated and deploying it to the resources was complicated.

For those who don't code, this is an inefficient, bug-prone scenario (except for a few, crazy extreme programming types who thrive in such an environment).

I decided to write my own visual script editor -- a tool that would help designers solve errors in their logic code before deploying it to resources. It was eventually deployed to all the other designers creating content on Baldur's Gate 2 and proved a rather useful tool.

After that I stopped getting bad reviews :)

CHAPTER 3 - Overcoming Obstacles

There is a wide range of obstacles you will encounter during your career. After summarizing some of the costs of videogame development (which influences how management communicates with their team and why companies make the decisions that they do) I will tackle how to handle specific issues that will arise during your career. These are not flaws or bugs in the game but are instead the various problems that arise from poor communication, ineffective meetings, rejection and crunch.

The Cost of Videogames

Modern videogames are incredibly costly. When I started with BioWare in 1999 there were around sixty employees spread over three projects. The design team on Baldur's Gate 2, my first videogame title, was fewer than 10. By the mid 2000s, on Dragon Age I was managing close to thirty designers... just the designers! The team itself was well over a hundred. The first cost of a modern triple A title is the overhead of having so many people.

A secondary cost is that with many games striving to ship with incredible and high quality art it becomes more difficult to be flexible with design. That is, once a particular design course is set, in regards to the actions available to players, it is costly to change that course. If you have decided that the main character cannot jump but then realize you need to add that ability there's thousands of animation and art assets that need to be recreated.

This previous is an obvious example, a less obvious one might be that design decides to add a new complement of (seemingly) simple powers... maybe the ability for the main player to throw fire. Even in this scenario, where existing animation might be utilized, it might be impossible to add this ability to an in-production game.

Why?

Let's pretend the rest of this hypothetical game is incredibly realistic -- with the ability to overturn cars, pick up and use items, drive vehicles, smash buildings, and so on. Because of the expectations set up elsewhere, many players would probably expect any powers in the game to behave realistically. If a fire ability is added they would expect it to cause materials to burn. To add a *burn state* for all art assets, after they have been created, is expensive.

Likewise, to tweak the combat balance on a game made ten years ago a designer just had to fiddle with numbers in a data file somewhere. Now actual animations may need to be adjusted, sometimes completely redone if there is a balancing issue. If you want somebody to punch slower in a fighting title, for example, several different groups need to work together to make that punch happen slower while still looking visually appropriate. They may also need to tweak the reactions of all the characters that could be hit by the ability!

Every line of dialog in a conversation in a Mass Effect or Dragon Age style game is a cutscene that has to take into account which party members might be with the player, the player's gender and the choices they have made previously. The area art has to be accounted for -- for example, what does the player see in the background of the conversation? Imagine what happens when a conversation is fine-tuned vocally and cinematically and then an artist adds a wall behind the conversation that cuts off the view of the horizon that the characters in the conversation are discussing! That conversation now has to be reworked cinematically.

When building large titles creating proof of concepts and prototypes and fully exploring the design requirements for the title is imperative before art and animation start creating the required resources.

The team itself is often the primary reason why costs escalate on projects. Not out of any malice or incompetence but sometimes the desire to always make the game *better* or to have every team member involved in all aspects of the game development process slows down development. I'll discuss this in the next two sections.

Cool - The Most Dangerous Word in Game Development

There used to be a joke around the BioWare office that whenever a coworker started a sentence with "Wouldn't it be cool if..." we would immediately reject the idea.

That might seem somewhat callous but the truth was (especially in later stages of development) there were far more *cool* ideas than *practical* ideas. The team could see the game's potential (a good thing) and wanted to improve it (also good). But as a manager it was important to know when to draw the line. And often if the best the team member could start with was "wouldn't it be cool..." then I became concerned about how much thought had gone into the new idea.

Evaluating the *coolness* of an idea is very difficult. You have to look at it from the point of the view of the player, in the context of how the game is intended to be played (i.e., some ideas are proposed because the in-progress game is not working the way it should... the idea makes sense until the game is complete... at which point it turns out to be unnecessary).

Also when evaluating a new idea I'd always want to know the impact on other departments (an idea that seems to impact designers mostly will still often have an art or animation impact). It is one thing to create work for your own department, another entirely to be adding tasks to other departments.

So, before you rush down to talk to your manager, take some time to work out not just how cool the idea is but its impact on everybody else. Have an idea of all the costs... it will make it easier for your manager to approve the idea.

> To be fair, on my early projects, I used to be the "wouldn't it be cool..." guy... always walking into the programmer's offices and throwing suggestions at them. Despite the fact that it might be nine or ten in the evening and everybody was wanting to go home. Learn from my mistakes. Please.

Too Many Bees

On larger games in larger companies the sheer size of the team works against itself. The more managers (and team members) the longer tasks take to complete. The workers who excelled at doing certain tasks end up becoming mid-level managers because the team size is too much for a single lead to effectively manage everybody.

The mid-level managers are no longer doing what they are good at. Much as I imagine it is like at most companies that have grown to a particular size.

Additionally, if the work environment is collaborate, that is, if everybody is encouraged to provide feedback and to work towards raising the quality bar on the title, the designers in particular can become overwhelmed with suggestions. Some of these suggestions, especially when delivered by senior members of other departments, often feel more like orders. A lot of scrambling is done, throughout the life cycle of the project, to incorporate all this feedback. Some of it is great, some of it is not... but all of it adds time to project schedules.

How to avoid this? I think setting a time and place for feedback is important. All departments should be encouraged to have open sessions... evaluation periods, if you will... where feedback is solicited (as described in the previous chapter). It should also be clear that when these sessions end, so also ends the time for feedback and change. This really works into the idea of a locking down content changes and other higher level management stuff. An obvious step to take but one that is difficult to implement in practicality.

But in general, I think giving everybody a time to offer feedback and to honestly assess that feedback, is fair. After that team members can still offer suggestions but it should be acknowledged that the likelihood of change has decreased radically. If a feature is working well and is fun and management is satisfied with it, it should be locked down. It could be made *better* but in all likelihood it is *good enough*.

Communication and Meetings

> Designers are the last line of communication. If nobody else is talking about a problem, a designer should start the dialog.

In general most *problems* I ran into on projects were caused by insufficient communication -- either management not explaining what they wanted, designers not explaining what the game was about, or artists not explaining what they could and could not build in the time frame. Inefficient and intrusive meetings and poorly written and scattered documentation also tended to create difficulties.

Communication, In General

Communication is a valuable skill, whether you communicate via bug reports, e-mail, one on one conversation or in larger meetings.

- **Say what you need to say and no more** Explain your ideas and your problems (and present possible solutions) with as little preamble and commentary as possible. Focus on the issue and not the distractions. Realize that whomever you are bringing the idea up to is as busy as you (or busier).

- **Be as Convincing as Possible** If you are certain that you have the next great idea and need to convince management, do your homework. Understand what they enjoy and what they hate. Spend far more time preparing for your discussion with them than you will spend in the actual discussion. Be prepared for every question, every objection. And at the end of the day do not dwell on lost battles... working in a team requires putting aside differences. No team has ever agreed on every issue.

- **Track it** If you feel the wrong decision has been made, make note of it, and if you feel strongly about it, track it -- user reactions, robustness, and such. But once a decision has been made do not try to reverse it unless you are firm in your conviction that not changing it will result in a flawed and failed game. Use the data you collect to help guide future decisions, either on this same game or on future titles you work on.

- **Use What You Have** When communicating use the methods the company has available. Creating a presentation with non-standard software that is not available for any other team member or in any meeting room is counter productive. Likewise don't use your own e-mail client, or your own home brew, inaccessible task management system. Part of effective communication is for all participants in a conversation to have equal grounding on the tools being used to communicate.

The Art of the Meeting

Meetings are important. They serve as a team bonding experience. They give everybody present in the meeting the opportunity to contribute to the issues being discussed.

But meetings are costly. The time spent in a meeting is time taken directly away from working on the game.

Here are some basic points to consider when setting up a meeting:

- **Participants** Invite only those that are needed for the meeting. Try to keep it under eight people. More than that is confusion.

- **Agenda** Meetings need to have an agenda. This should be a short summary of what the meeting is about and who is attending. Attach supporting documentation. Suggest to those attending that they discuss the agenda with their own groups before the meeting, to solicit ideas or concerns. This helps keeps any particular meeting from growing too large but also ensures that the majority of the team has at least some level of involvement.

- **Be Realistic in the time** Plan to end your meeting ten minutes before the hour. In a busy company some employees have meetings stacked up all day. When a meeting runs late it impacts every other meeting. Avoid this.

The participants are as important to a successful meeting as the meeting coordinator is. There is an etiquette to how everybody should operate in a meeting which includes giving everybody present the opportunity to speak, not going on the defensive (or offensive) but remaining open to all ideas while ensuring that both the positive and negative aspects of a particular point are explored. It also means showing respect to both the meeting organizer and the rest of the team involved.

Distraction Devices

Do not use your phone, pda, laptop or other electronic device during a meeting. Do not even look at it, unless it is to contribute something to the meeting (or to read a digital copy of the supplemental material for the meeting... though of course you should have read that *before* the meeting).

In the later stages of my career I noticed a proliferation of portable devices being used during meetings. It was happening all the time.

Ten people in a room discussing a cool feature, or trying to plan a demo and half of them had their noses buried in their portable devices catching up on email, or messages, or whatever. When I was working on Neverwinter Nights in the mid-2000s we only had a handful of meetings a week, and seldom needed to revisit decisions four or five times but on later projects I was finding that we were having a handful of meetings a day and often the meetings were repeats, going over decisions that had already been made.

Now this isn't *entirely* the fault of using these distraction devices but I cannot help think that some were leaving the meetings not entirely sure of what had been decided -- because they were *not paying attention*. More than once a senior coworker on the project came into my office asking why we had decided X,Y,Z when they had actually been present for the meeting that made that decision!

So, as a shout out to those of you new to industry -- do not do this. Multi-tasking is highly inefficient. And besides, didn't you enter the game industry to be actually involved in making games? Be involved.

Too Many Meetings?

This is more of a suggestion for the entire company. If management has every day solidly booked with meetings the company is doing something wrong. Management needs to be available to deal with the issues arising on the project. Not always meeting.

Now many would argue that meetings are essential and they might even religiously defend each and every appointment on their calendar. Sometimes they might even be right. But if I were to do an audit of a project looking for inefficiencies I would start by examining their meeting schedules.

First I would look to see if meetings are being held to revisit decisions already made. Is this some sign that management is weak and too willing to make changes at every turn? Has there been management overturn on the project? If duplicate meetings can be trimmed time will be freed up on the schedule. This requires the project to have a strong roadmap for how development should work. And they should stick to it, not reversing decisions unless absolutely necessary.

Secondly I would insist that there be meeting free periods, perhaps *no meetings in the morning...* and make this company wide. Interruption creates poor performance... meetings are an interruption (even if at times, a necessary one).

E-mail

In this age of social networking and messenging I still feel e-mail plays a vital role in communication. Effectively e-mail is small-scale documentation of what is happening on a project. While in a later book I will detail some effective (and some ineffective) documentation strategies I have employed over the years here I focus on some ways to make your e-mail more readable and how to avoid making embarrassing mistakes.

Short!

E-mail should be short. But comprehensive. The e-mail can have links to larger documentation but the gist of the information should be present in the e-mail itself. The reader should be able to respond to the e-mail. (As should you! If you receive a request to review documentation you should tell the sender when you will have time to do so and add it to your schedule.)

E-mail is often ignored

You should never ignore e-mail sent to you. But you should also learn why your e-mail might be being ignored. I learned to avoid certain dead zones in regards to sending out e-mail. Basically there are certain periods of time where people were too busy to respond to e-mail.

Monday mornings seemed the worst... people were back from a weekend and many seemed to purge their outstanding e-mails as quickly as they could without reading them (presumably to start the week with a clean slate.) By Monday afternoon employees were caught up and important e-mail had a chance of receiving a response. Another dead period was Friday afternoons. Everybody was ramping up for the weekend and nobody wanted to be handed a major issue right before they left. So they avoided their e-mail. Friday e-mails were doubly doomed because Friday e-mail often became victims in the Monday purge.

You Copied this to Whom?

One day I received an e-mail from an editor, the contents of which are unimportant, but what *is* important is that the editor did a carbon copy of the email to dozens of other authors (using the carbon copy, or cc field, in their e-mail program).

The problem with this is that I now have the e-mail addresses for a bunch of writers, some of which, like myself, use a private e-mail address for professional correspondence. Now, it's not the worse thing in the world for other writers to have access to these addresses but it was still a breach of each writer's privacy.

I've seen the same thing happen back when I dayjobbed -- an e-mail is forwarded but includes e-mail information about senior company members to a third party, releasing what might be sensitive contact information outside the company.

This is where the blind carbon copy, or BCC, comes in. E-mail programs include a BCC field. When you use it, the e-mail addresses are hidden from the other recipients when the e-mail is sent!

Do Not Address This

Another little e-mail tip I have is that you should never put the e-mail addresses of the people you intend to send the e-mail to into the e-mail until you are ready to send the e-mail.

Why?

This prevents two errors, one trivial, one serious. The trivial error is that you accidentally press send before you are finished composing the e-mail. If this happens once or twice, nobody cares. If you do it all the time... well depending on the work environment you might find yourself the butt of jokes for years to come. I've seen it happen.

The more serious issue is that if you are writing an e-mail out of anger or frustration you do not want your first draft to be read. Especially accidentally. You want to give yourself time to walk away, calm down, and compose a more appropriate and diplomatic second draft. Trust me, the first draft, angry e-mail is never effective.

Failing and Fixing

You will make mistakes. It is inevitable. But it is also vital that you learn how to respond to criticism and rejection and how to correct your mistakes, timely and efficiently.

Rejection

The kinds of rejection you might experience while working vary on your position. As a programmer you might have a way to refactor the existing code for a game that is ready to ship that will make code maintenance easier but be told by management that there is not time to implement changes. A designer might be deflated when their idea for an exciting story-arc is refused.

These are two easy examples with which I can explain why the rejection happened in the first place.

For the programmer in the later stages of a project a code change that would make the game run faster or more efficiently is valuable but a change to make future changes easier, while logical, is not something management will often sign off on. Near the end of the game development cycle the focus is on getting the game out of the door. Not making behind-the-scenes changes. The code refactoring suggestion would be better timed when work begins on the sequel.

Likewise there's no time to make radical changes to plots in the last few months leading up to ship. Even if the writing changes could be made and the level art required created there would not be enough time to bring in new voice actors and push the voice resources into the game.

So in both cases these rejections were inevitable.

So really, the first rule of avoiding rejections is to understand the timing of your suggestions and this will only happen with a little experience as every studio will vary in their expectations.

Learn from Rejection

Another form of rejection is when your actual content is criticized. Basically you'll become a stronger developer if you understand *why* you are being told to change what you are doing. Talk to your peers and ask if they have received similar feedback in the past. If they have, how did they respond to the criticisms? What changes did they make?

Even if you do not, at an artistic level, agree with the changes, realize that you may not be able to do things your way until you have proven yourself. Understand what your managers want you to do and to satisfy their requirements.

Inconsistent Rejection

Sometimes rejection just happens because there is not enough time in the schedule to finish things. This is the easiest rejection to accept because it has nothing to do with the quality of your work.

But there's a lesson to be learned here as well. Are you always having your work cut? Sometimes it might be no fault of your own but if it happens often you should question whether you are delivering your content as fast as is needed. If not, think about ways to improve the process -- perhaps you need better design specifications up front or a better computer or more time to plan?

Squashing Bugs

You should handle your bugs like you do your e-mail. Every company uses different software to track bugs, or defects, in their games but most allow the bug recipient to add comments to the bug as they work on it. You should do this.

Do not allow bugs to sit on your list for weeks without explanation. If you are stuck in fixing the bug, explain why and what you need (obviously if this issue is a major issue you should be speaking to your manager but with minor issues a simple explanation added to the bug is often sufficient). This commentary helps management understand you have looked into the issue and are simply waiting for new resources.

If a bug is fixed mark it as such so that it can be retested.

And always evaluate the final fix you have made to an issue and see if it invalidates previous fixes. Imagine a scenario where you cannot make a door unlock after the player has performed all the correct steps. You finally construct a hack that forces the door open and this works. But then weeks later programming fixes a core issue in the engine that has been affecting all doors (making them all difficult to open). Your previous fix is now no longer needed. You should remove the hack to prevent your *fix* from introducing side effects into the game (the caveat to this is that late on a project it might be better not to touch anything, even to remove unneeded data like this... as removing the unneeded fix might break something else!)

Crunch - Dread Nemesis or Surprise Ally?

Designers do not hate crunch. Designers embrace crunch, because it means they get to design more.

Working overtime (or crunchtime or game development hell, depending on the person talking about it) is a given in the video game industry. Though during my years with BioWare crunchtime was significantly reduced as scheduling methods improved, it still remained a necessary evil. This section focuses on how to make the most, as an employee, of the overtime you will be working.

Your First Crunch

I keep a journal and though I am not consistent with updating it anymore I looked over some old entries I had made during the crunch I served on Baldur's Gate II. One sentence I wrote was the following:

This is definitely the strangest time on a project.

I still agree with this statement. Crunch, whether it is handled poorly or turned into a strong bonding experience for the team, is always a little strange. There you are working away into the late hours... the time of night when sane humans are out at the movies or partying or sleeping. Instead you are adding seven new types of demon to the database or fixing a texture issue or debugging a plot that seems determined to work opposite of what you intended.

Crunch sometimes felt to me like a house party that refused to end... always somebody lingering in the hallway well after everybody should have went home. But good crunches were also *fun*, and an opportunity to bond with the others on the team working late. I interacted more with departments outside of design during crunch than I ever did during normal working hours. And I learned more too... not just about how to make a great game but also about the kinds of people who make a game great.

A Bad Crunch

Some overtime is inevitably unpleasant. Perhaps your manager has announced one of the lame kinds of crunch -- maybe forcing everybody to scan a hundred thousand lines of dialog and remove the letter 'k'. How do you make it better?

Take breaks. Wander the halls. Talk to coworkers you do not normally talk to, even the creepy guy who insists on wearing his bathrobe at 2am. Realize that everybody else is stressed out. Do not take anything personally -- if a bug is introduced just fix it. Blame and accountability and improving workflow can all be handled later... the wee hours of the morning are not the time for that.

Eat fruits and vegetables. Yeah I know that's not what you want to hear but if you are in a long-term crunch lasting weeks, if not months, you need to be eating healthy. Keep the coffee and sweet snacks to a minimum.

And bring enough food to share. Sharing makes cranky tired workers happy.

Goof off occasionally. Sending out the occasional amusing e-mail or sitting with the team and talking about what's going on in their lives is important. Taking the job too seriously makes it more stressful and while it is important to act like a professional (getting tasks done on time and to quality while being respectful to co-workers), you also need to have a bit of fun or else you won't enjoy the job.

If you find yourself working sympathy crunch, in that even though you have no bugs of your own to take care of, do not be pissed off about it. Play the game and enjoy it for what it is, a game you helped build! If that's not enough to make you happy then be satisfied that every bug you send will make a coworker more miserable. (Though do try to be constructive.)

A Good Crunch?

So what is a good crunch? The best crunches, in my opinion, are the ones where the team, together, is aiming towards a common goal -- a demo candidate or a release candidate or even just one completed level that functions exactly as it should in the final game.

These are the ones I still remember fondly... trying for a release candidate on a game, sending each candidate out to the publisher and quickly squashing the bugs when it came back rejected. Everybody on the team could orient themselves towards that tangible goal and it was a common ground that could be talked about during breaks.

It created camaraderie, the entire team sharing the disappointment of a rejected candidate but ultimately rejoicing when a release finally passed... which meant the game had been accepted, which meant all the hard work over the months and years leading to that moment would soon be rewarded by having actual real gamers play your game. That's the best crunch.

And...

Make crunchtime work for you; try to get the most of it. Obviously if your team or your company constantly turns to crunch as a solution for poor scheduling you need to be thinking about how to improve scheduling or moving to another studio. But when crunch is handled responsibly, it can be a fun and creative experience.

When I look over my journal of my crunch time on Neverwinter Nights and Baldur's Gate 2 I see phrases like *awesome*, *fulfilling*, and *worthwhile*.

So go enjoy your overtime!

Summary

So ends the first book in the Lazy Designer series. I hope it serves as a useful primer for the early months and years of your game development career. Later books will go into more detail on specific areas that have been discussed only in general terms here with sections on prototyping, rapid iteration, scheduling, designing fun levels, building worlds, making hard managerial decisions and developing innovative and compelling storylines and characters.

> Baldur's Gate 2 was released September 2000, just a year after I had started my career at BioWare. I won't ever forget how proud I was to walk into a store and see a game I had helped make on the shelves. Even as a junior designer I felt I had made a contribution to BG2 and will always remember that first year fondly.

As a bonus and a preview of the content future Lazy Designer books will contain, here's a section from a chapter out of Book Two.

Designing Frustration

Over the years I have tried several task management solutions... from Excel to Outlook to Google Tasks and many more. Currently I'm back to using Excel sheets again to keep track of which blog posts need writing, what writing projects I want to tackle next. But tasks written there continually accumulate.

Beside my laptop I also have a pile of sticky notes. If I am away from the computer when a task presents itself I usually jot it down on a note. And I have discovered something. Those paper tasks are generally completed faster than digitally-tracked tasks!

Likewise I have hundreds of unread books stored digitally... and while I do read them my progress through digital copy is significantly slower than my progress through the variety of paper books and magazines I own.

I recently finished reading one of those magazines (Neo-Opsis #20). In it Karl Johanson, the editor (who also works in the game industry) commented that game designers should add _just enough frustration_ to a game to keep the player playing.

So, what's my point?

These three seemingly separate ideas -- task management with sticky notes, reading paper versus digital books, and frustration designing -- are not separate at all. Frustration management is vital to game design... and real life.

Basically the reason I tackle my sticky note tasks before I look at my task list in Excel is because the sticky notes are *frustrating*. They linger on my desk, my monitor, my wall. They take up space. They annoy me. They frustrate me. I want to complete them so that I can crumple them up and toss them to the floor.

Likewise the books... those stacks of unread material stare at me every time I enter or leave my office. They beg to be read. Digital devices have convenient features that allow me to suppress their notifications and ignore them when I want... notes and books do not allow that luxury. Their sheer presence demands attention.

Digital reminders and eBooks do not frustrate (most of) us with their presence. Neither do many games. Anybody designing product for a digital environment should seriously consider that some frustrations are necessary... frustrations force a user to pay attention, to engage.

Game Design Frustrations

Game design frustrations should lead to in-game player choices (frustrations that the player cannot remove are poor design.)

I think an example might illustrate effective use of game frustrations.

A common feature of old RPGs is the idea of a limited inventory. Basically the player is allowed to carry a limited amount of equipment. Certain RPG designers, in an attempt to make their games appeal to mainstream crowds have removed the system or attempted to simplify it.

One simplification has been to expand the inventory available to the player (sometimes so much so that the inventory becomes infinite). The solution works, to a degree, but an infinite inventory introduce new problems... larger inventories become difficult for a player to navigate, for example.

Worse... the designer has now lost an opportunity to make a system enhance gameplay. Sure a frustration has been removed but the player was not active in removing the frustration (lost gameplay) and the replacement simply introduces a new frustration (which also adds no new gameplay).

Sometimes frustrations must be removed to fit into the overall design of a game but I think it is a design oversight to make too many simplifications simply for the sake of simplification.

Inventory is an easy concept for non-RPG players to understand. A limited inventory also makes *sense*. The more a game mechanic models a real life situation (i.e., I can only carry so much in my backpack/briefcase/whatever) the easier it is for a player to understand how it should work. When a player encounters a full inventory (a frustration) it is simple for them to think of solutions to their frustration.

They know they can:

1. **Return to a Previous Area** There they can sell excess equipment -- which encourages exploring existing areas and creates an opportunity for a game designer to add simple dialog and other cues to reinforce the player's influence on the world.

2. **Expand or Organize Their Inventory** This might encourage the player to undertake subplots or find specialist merchants who will sell them expensive methods to upgrade their inventory (magical backpacks, houses, starships -- whatever makes sense in the context of the world being explored).

Basically a game system (inventory) has the power to encourage *exploration* and heighten the player's sense of control over their game experience.

Other examples abound -- perhaps fighting mobs of weak opponents becomes boring at higher levels. Why not encourage the player to take a side route (or a series of ever more dangerous side routes) to obtain an artifact that gives the player the ability to destroy those mobs more quickly?

If a particular opponent is difficult to defeat maybe there is a weapon that can be bought at high cost that will vanquish it more efficiently -- the expense requiring the player to undertake several subplots to raise the funds required.

Even if these subplots are simple, if done correctly, they make the player feel like they are making *decisions* and are not being forced down a singular path. Encourage exploration of the world, and revisiting existing areas... but do not make it tedious.

It is a balancing act. The player needs to be encouraged to reduce the frustration but in most cases the game should still be playable *without* reducing the frustration.

When Frustration is Frustrating

Frustration does not mean difficult or awkward to play. If the gameplay is extremely obtuse it is likely that some players will quit playing the game -- or not play it in the first place if negative word of mouth reaches them before they purchase.

Many designers will say systems like limited inventory, party management, and games with too many choices are the frustrations that stop mainstream players from enjoying more complicated titles.

I disagree.

Bad design stops mainstream players from enjoying these games. You cannot recycle gameplay elements and throw them together in a jumbled design and expect players to embrace the game. As a lead designer I've fallen prey to this trap many times myself, assuming every player would *just get it*.

Beware of *murkiness*. These are places in the design where a player hits a frustration and *does not understand* how to minimize that frustration. This is not a problem with the feature itself. It is a problem of presentation.

This is a very real issue with designing traditional role playing games. Designers *assume* the audience understands all the terms, the history, and the expectations that come from this style of game. These game features will work for modern players but only if incorporated into a strong design framework. This will take time, effort, play testing and iteration.

You might ask: to save time and energy why not remove the frustration in the first place?

If you take out all the frustrations you diminish the player's experience. There becomes fewer opportunities for them to take an active role in their experience. Lose all frustrations and you do not have a game.

Designing Good Frustration

Teach players to solve problems and they will enjoy the game. There is nothing fundamentally confusing about an RPG but expecting a new player to jump into a genre that has had decades of development and just *get it* is short-sighted.

When players complain about repetitious, boring combat or uninspired levels or a flat progression system, it is likely that there are not enough opportunities for players to solve problems. Your game needs more frustration!

Likewise, when a game mechanic or rules system frustration crops up in play testing as a bug, do consider other solutions than simply cutting it. There might be an inexpensive option that not only reduces the frustration but also increases the player's sense of control and ownership over the game they are playing.

It is just going to take talented designers to figure out how to present these frustrations in a way that enhances gameplay.

Emotional Narratives and Frustration

An emotional narrative is a story within a game that is built with the intention of a player reaching ever escalating moments of emotional involvement. Basically it is a game experience that mirrors the experience a movie might provide.

In these types of games it can be argued that frustrations, especially ones that lead the player away from the main storyline arc (or lead them to complete it in a non-standard way in which the emotional punch can't be delivered) are *bad things*.

And they are.

Allowing the player to go off and deal with *trivial* things like obtaining a cool new sword, or a method of fast travel, or searching for a trainer to complete a level-up, these are all distractions. If enough time is spent away from the main emotional narrative 'track', the emotional affect will be diluted.

But I see games with such tight arcs of expectation as interactive movies. I can play them and enjoy them but some are trending away from being *games*, or at least the sorts of games I love building and playing, at all. I worry when I see the phrase *emotional arc* in game design documents. It comes with too many expectations and assumptions.

In a linear game (with few choices) it is easy to construct an emotional arc. In a game with significant player choice this becomes a larger challenge. Often the solution, no matter the starting intent of the designers, will be to simplify that path by removing choices.

Surprise Frustrations

I would be cautious about throwing out too many unexpected surprises. Little surprises that work within the existing and expected gameplay framework are awesome but big surprises that invalidate all the learning and time the player has put into the game are dangerous.

In the games I have worked on where levels or sections of the game have had their gameplay radically altered (player's equipment taken away or powers lost or new powers temporarily gained) there has generally been a negative player backlash. *Some* players really enjoy the abrupt change but many become annoyed. Adjusting to the new experience has become too frustrating for them and in some cases they feel like they are playing an entirely different game, not the one they had been enjoying up until that moment.

The exception of course would be the game that is entirely full of unexpected events. I was able to enjoy Indigo Prophecy because from the beginning I was trained to realize that gameplay would constantly be changing on me. That was the nature of that experience... I did not become invested in one style of gameplay because I knew it would change. Had it instead started out as a traditional adventure game and then three quarters through radically changed the way controls worked, I would have been *too frustrated.*

A (Frustratingly Fun) RPG Game Overview

I will end this section now with a bit of an overview of how I might use frustration to build a RPG. The caveat to this of course is that this is all theoretical and like all things living in the land of theory may or may not be successful in the marketplace. I would have to build a prototype first and experiment with some of the suggestions that follow before investing time or effort into fully fleshing the idea out.

Imagine you have a fairly limited area budget (say 10-15 environments) and need to build a 200 hour roleplaying game. How to do this?

I would try to (wisely) use frustration to expand the available gameplay.

First I would make the environments have four or five key points of differentiation. This has nothing to do with frustration of course but as a designer I want my players to feel some sense of exploration. Fifteen areas that all feature the same type of forest, for example, is not fun exploration. Journeying from deep catacombs to an underwater city to great plains to a small town... more fun. Different art themes creates exploration.

> *The more art themes a game has the fewer areas you are going to receive because each theme adds to the development costs.*

We will have a progression system. Here is a great opportunity to introduce fun frustration. While no designer wants to remove the concept of a level up (when a player reaches a new power plateau) I would suggest the following:

- **Automatic Power** Have some passive properties of the player improve automatically at level up. These might include the player's health or the number of spells available to them.
- **Trainers** The player will be forced to seek out trainers to improve active abilities (such as learning a new spell or improving an existing one)

This limitation on acquiring a new power could be frustrating to a player but the benefit is that, through earlier explorations, they will have met some trainers and have some leads on where they might need to travel when they require new training. A player might know of two different trainers -- a fire magic trainer and an ice magic trainer -- and be forced to make a choice depending on the progression path they want to take on which to visit.

So we have a trainer frustration introduced. Combined with the need for players to visit stores scattered across our limited world to improve their weapons/armor and to sell their loot, the player has a lot of traveling in their future.

A benefit of revisiting areas is that the designer gets to present a changing world to players, a world impacted by the player's actions.

So we make sure we introduce new content to existing areas, within our limited budget, and players receive additional rewards and opportunities for interaction beyond the main reason for revisiting areas (find a trainer or use a store). But maybe over time the player still gets bored (frustrated) with fighting hordes of creatures that are now too easy for them to defeat but still time-consuming.

We have created a new frustration. What can we do? Well we won't be scaling the creatures to improve their challenge (I detest creature scaling... more on that in another chapter). Instead we introduce a few magical artifacts that will influence how players use their spells. Maybe near the beginning of the game players only have access to direct-attack spells that harm one target (a bolt of fire, a stream of ice) but after finding particular artifacts they can actually change how their spells work as required... a *fire bolt* becomes a *fire ball*. It might do less damage but it can wipe out a mob of critters quickly.

The player has reduced their frustration... but of course now the player has more traveling to do... and this is another frustration.

Even with introducing growth to existing areas (new dialog reactions to what the player has accomplished previously and random combat encounters) players may start becoming frustrated with traveling back and forth across areas they have already seen. The thrill of exploration is lost once an area is revisited too often. So we introduce the *opportunity* for a player to earn the means to fast travel.

Fast travel is the ability to use an overhead map to rapidly transition from one location to another, usually instantly. The player does not have to manually walk across the areas she has already visited.

Weak design would simply unlock fast travel at a point for all players. A more interesting design requires the player to obtain the means and method of fast travel. Depending on the game this could mean purchasing (or finding) a horse, a car, a dragon or even a spaceship. Maybe there are ways to improve the speed of existing vehicles. Let the player solve the problem... choosing when to spend their money (and how to earn that money), or when to adventure in search of the vehicle and where possible *which* vehicle.

The player reduces their own frustration.

As a designer we have accomplished our goal. Because we have kept some frustrations in our core gameplay players now have reason to revisit every area in your game and with a little extra effort you will make those visits even more rewarding!

Thank You!

I was honored to have worked with many great game designers, artists and programmers throughout my years with BioWare. To all of them I owe a sincere *thank you*, for the experiences we shared -- good, bad, and generally hilarious -- and for what they taught me.

I would also like to thank a few co-workers, specifically.

James Ohlen and Kevin Martens, who are both still very active in the gaming industry, were my first mentors and I will always appreciate their patience and openness in discussing what I was doing right and what I needed to improve and for giving me amazing opportunities.

On Neverwinter Nights the lead tools programmer, Don Moar, spent countless hours with me, not only working with me to work out the design for the now legendary Neverwinter Nights toolset, but his advice also influenced my design processes and my own, personal, software projects.

David Gaider, Drew Karpyshyn, and the other BioWare writers have influenced my storytelling a great deal. Though we seldom sat down and discussed writing directly I learned much from studying their storytelling methods.

Preston Watamaniuk, Georg Zoeller and Yaron Jakobs taught me so much about rules design, creating rock-solid systems and improving user experience. Any designer would be blessed to have worked with one of these designers, I had the opportunity to work on multiple titles with all three.

Finally, my thanks go out to Cori May who, upon learning of my retirement, sent out a kind e-mail to the staff at BioWare summarizing my game design philosophies, many of those notes have appeared as blurbs throughout this text. Additional thanks to Don, Cori, and game designer/reviewer Bob McCabe for their many insightful comments and encouragements on my blog. These are much appreciated!

And of course, thanks to my ever patient family for giving me the time I need to write what I must.

Links

Here are a few links, some referenced in the text, some added to help guide you in your own explorations.

Further Reference Material

I've read the **iPhone Developer's Cookbook** (http://www.amazon.ca/exec/obidos/ASIN/0321555457/) and **iPhone Game Development** (http://www.amazon.ca/exec/obidos/ASIN/0596159854/)and thought that both did a good job of walking a reader through the steps needed to build an application/game. Plenty of examples in both though all are geared towards someone with programming experience. I discuss them a bit on my blog (http://blog.brentknowles.com/2009/12/07/iphone-game-development/).

As well I enjoyed **Fundamentals of Game Design** (http://www.amazon.ca/Fundamentals-Game-Design-Ernest-Adams/dp/0131687476/)by Ernest Adams and Andrew Rollings. If you have little idea of what goes into making video games, the actual concrete terms and methodology of constructing games, this is a good title to review.

There are many great tutorials out there. When learning flash this tutorial (http://www.emanueleferonato.com/2006/12/06/flash-game-creation-tutorial-part-3)was of great use for me. The tutorial's creator has also developed tutorials for HTML5 and other systems.

A few BioWare co-workers have started blogs. If you are curious about checking in on the activities of professional game designers, here's some links for you:

- **IndyAlpha** http://indyalpha.blogspot.com/
- **Trent Oster** http://www.trentoster.com/
- **Bob McCabe** http://gamergranola.trickybuddha.com/
- **Rob Bartel** http://robbartel.blogspot.com/

Ten Years At BioWare

And for those of you who would like to explore what working at BioWare for ten years was like, I broke my experiences there into ten parts.

Start reading here:

Year 1 http://blog.brentknowles.com/2009/08/25/bioware-brent-year-1-1999/

Lazy Designer Series

If you would like to know when the next book in the Lazy Designer series is available please consider **subscribing** to my blog at blog.brentknowles.com or the official lazy designer site at lazydesigner.brentknowles.com. I will only spam you a little bit.

Glossary

Avatar A virtual representation of the player. Generally the character you are controlling when playing a video game.

Batch files These are text files that contain a list of commands that can all be executed at once. Generally used on resource pipelines for games to automate repetitious procedures when preparing a game build.

Digital distribution Selling software over the Web, instead of in a retail package. This can include selling a full game digitally or offering add-ons to an existing title (new items, new abilities, new levels to explore.)

Flash This is a web-based technology for creating games and other multimedia presentations. Flash is a great starter for those wanting to learn the basics of game design but not all devices support flash playback.

Hack Generally a programming or scripting tweak to force an aspect of gameplay work, but not in an elegant or maintainable way. Hacks are usually introduced in the late stages of game development when it is too dangerous to modify the core behavior of a game industry. An example might be that the game engine loses track of NPCs after a while and they stop behaving... if the problem was discovered too late in the development cycle, fixing it could invalidate all the testing for the entire game engine. An alternative might be to hack in a fix at the scripting (designer) level of gameplay that forces NPCs to remind the engine that they still exist.

Intellectual property (IP) This is a label generally referring to a game franchise and/or the world a game is set in. Sometimes game companies license a popular game franchise (like Star Wars) to make a video game for.

Intranet An internal network, like the Web but able to be viewed only by employees at a company. Useful for posting information everyone needs to know about, including game documentation.

Level up This terms is generally used in role-playing games and refers to when a player is able to increase the power of their avatar. By advancing through the game, defeating opponents and completing quests, the player increases their experience points. Once these experiences points reach certain areas the player earns a level up, an increase in power.

Machinima The use of real-time 3D computer graphics to create cinematic productions. Several cinematic designers working at BioWare came from the machima community.

Mods These are levels built for existing games by fans of the game. They are generally add-ons, giving more exploration to the original game, or telling a parallel story. Occasionally they are complete redoes of the game... using the core game interface but setting it in a different world. Mods are usually accomplished by using a toolset supplied by the games manufacturer.

Non-linear narrative Games should encourage players to make choices and these choices makes games very different from books and movies. In a non-linear game the player dictates where they go and when and in what order.

Non-player characters (NPCS) These are computer controlled creatures. They may be your allies or your enemies or non-combatants in a videogame.

Real time strategy games (RTSs) The popular Blizzard title Starcraft is probably the most successful RTS. These games involve the player controlling large numbers of units in massive military campaigns against other players (or computer controlled teams).

Role-playing games (RPGs) Role-playing games that generally combine a strong story-arc with player customization and a progression system. Players often control more than one character at a time, utilizing small squads or parties to engage in tactical combat.

Scripter A designer that takes dialog, locations, creatures and makes them all function as a virtual game world. This generally involves write programming code, though generally a lighter weight code called a scripting language.

Wiki A website hosted on a company's intranet that allows employees to add topics and discuss them. Great for interactive documentation.

About the Author

Brent Knowles is a writer, programmer, and game designer.

A graduate of the University of Alberta's computer science program. Brent worked for the role-playing game developer BioWare for ten years where he was a scripter/writer on Baldur's Gate 2 before transitioning to a lead design position on Neverwinter Nights, working on both the core game and the two expansions that followed. He also did combat design for the console title Jade Empire and eventually became lead designer for Dragon Age: Origins.

After retiring from BioWare Brent began game consulting for various companies, including the social stock market Empire Avenue and writing fiction full time.

Brent has over twenty stories and articles published in a variety of magazines and anthologies (including Dragon Magazine, On Spec, and Pyramid). In 2009 Brent placed first in the third quarter of the Writer's of the Future Contest with his story 'Digital Rights'.

#

If you enjoyed book 1 of the Lazy Designer, check out the other books in the series by visiting **lazydesigner.brentknowles.com**.

Connect with me:
Twitter: http://www.twitter.com/brent_knowles
Email: Subscribe to my mailing list (and maybe win freebies)
http://blog.brentknowles.com/subscribe/
Amazon: http://www.amazon.com/Brent-Knowles/e/B0035WW7OW
Facebook: http://www.facebook.com/#!/KnowlesBrent

Made in the USA
San Bernardino, CA
06 January 2014